BETWEEN THE HILLS
"PICKENS HOLLOW"
A MEMOIR

DEBORAH LEDFORD WOODARD

Summary: A family memoir of life on a large Middle Tennessee farm from the Depression to post World War II.

ISBN: 978-1-7335521-4-1

On the Cover

The Ledford home on the Middle Tennessee farm. It was built circa 1800s. The home is still standing dramatic, elegant and preserved.

It is said that Louie Armstrong always signed his autographs "Red Beans and Ricely Yours." When asked why he did this he stated, "Because I don't want to forget my roots."

This book is dedicated to my sweet Aunt Linda who envisioned a compilation of memoirs...

A memoir of life in Pickens Hollow.

Ledford Coat of Arms

Prologue

All the "Aunts" were born before 1952. I know this because I was born in 1952. This was the year that Harry S. Truman was President, and Dwight Eisenhower would win the Presidential election and go on to serve for 1953-1961.

All the Aunts were born in the South. In the South, strong women persevere regardless of the odds. Whether they were aware of this is not known. It was just something they did...in the DNA...one foot in front of the other.

The South was largely agricultural until the mid-1940's. The Aunts were all born on large working farms. For one reason or another, death or war, men were not always present. There was no mystique here. All the Aunts had to grab hold and work even scratching their very essence into the dirt. Although in the years ahead each Aunt would be uniquely their own, they had all looked out the same window.

Memoirs of Pickens Hollow

Sometimes, it's funny what is laid in our laps. Granddaddy always said he would never worry about Aunt Amy after he saw her drive, no matter where her destination. So, it is with this book. I can't glimpse the destination, but please go with us on our journey and adventure as we will be driving on.

Middle Tennessee is Heaven on Earth for many. Even those who moved away left their hearts there. This verdant area is known for its beautiful rolling hills and valleys with streams. Nashville, the state capitol, is also in the area. Tennessee is such a wide state that it is divided into East, Middle, and West. Middle Tennessee is the largest area.

Middle Tennessee was originally settled by Native Americans. These people grew corn, wheat and tobacco. This area continues to be agricultural.

The Aunts lived in Southern Middle Tennessee known for its scenic beauty and southern hospitality. Famous are the Tennessee Walking Horses. These horses were first used on farms and plantations. They then became popular in the show rings, in movies, on television and were used for performances.

Plentiful were the working farms and plantations in this area. The Aunts lived on a large working farm. Notable was that Andrew Jackson had a plantation farm in this area named Hermitage where cotton was king. Like Hermitage, the Aunts' farm had orchards, cattle and sheep.

The Aunts lived in a beautiful place "between the hills" called Pickens Hollow. Pickens Hollow is a valley in Marshall County, Tennessee. The elevation is approximately 728 feet.

Names and traditions were important. The Pickens' name can be traced back to the 1800's. Work was revered, and these individuals were strong and resourceful. These individuals had deep roots. Families were tight knit and interwoven with other neighboring families for social and economic needs and survival.

Growing up the Aunts saw fall harvests, winter moons, beautiful snows and summer grass. There were spring plantings, seeds grown into the good earth and streams replenished by the strong rains. They so loved the animals that "abided" with them.

When they were grown and gone, their hearts still yearned for the land of their beloved Pickens Hollow.

The working farm was over 1000 acres. Work was hard, but the food was always bountiful in the seasons. There were meats, fresh and cured. There were chickens, turkeys, vegetables and fruits from the orchards.

"Dame" Grandmother Ruth had to feed many mouths including family, workers, worker's families and "Frog" and his family. Grandmother Ruth was a "Black Skillet Artist." In her black skillet, she could prepare the entree, vegetables, breads and desserts. She was so efficient with her skills that this was accomplished in warp speed.

Favorite Recipes

Chess Pie

3 Eggs
1 Stick Butter
1 Tbsp. Vinegar
1 1/2 Cups Sugar
1 Tbsp. Meal
1 tsp. Vanilla

Cream butter and sugar then add eggs and beat. Add meal and continue to mix while adding vinegar and vanilla. Pour into a 9-inch pie crust and bake at 350 degrees for 50 minutes.

Black Skillet Peach Cobbler

We had our own peach orchard so when peaches were in season Mama made cobbler about every day. She would make the cobbler in a black skillet. Start by putting the crust on the bottom and baking for a few minutes. Then put the peach mixture in and cover with another crust. Cut a few slits in the top, and cover with a little sugar and butter and bake.

Peach Mixture
6-8 Peaches
1 1/2 Cups Sugar
Put into crust. Bake at 375 degrees for 45 minutes.
Mama made her own crust with flour, water, lard, sugar, and salt.

Old Fashioned Raisin Pie

2 Cups Raisins
2 Cups Water
1/2 Cup Brown Sugar
2 Tbsp. Corn Starch
1/2 tsp. Cinnamon
1/4 tsp. Salt
1 Tbsp. Vinegar
1 Tbsp. Butter or Oleo
Pastry for 1 Crust

Combine raisins and water. Boil 5 minutes. Blend sugar, cornstarch, cinnamon and salt. Add to raisins and cook, stirring until clear.
Remove from heat. Stir in vinegar and butter. Cool slightly. Pour into pie crust and cover with lattice strips. Bake at 425 degrees for 30 minutes or until golden brown.

Skillet Fried Corn

White corn preferred.
Cut corn off the cobs and milk the cobs. Fry bacon in black skillet until crisp. Remove bacon but save the drippings in the skillet. Stir in the corn. Cook 8-10 minutes. Add water or sweet milk if desired to prevent corn from becoming too dry. Top with bacon.

Skillet Fried Apples

6-8 Tart Cooking Apples, cored and sliced
1 Stick of Butter
Juice 1/2 Lemon
1/4 Cup Light brown Sugar
Dash of Cinnamon or Nutmeg

Add apples to melted butter and coat. Sprinkle with lemon juice, brown sugar and cinnamon or nutmeg. Cover tightly and cook for 10 minutes.

Skillet Cornbread

1/4 Cup Oil, Shortening or Bacon Fat
2 Cups Self-Rising Cornmeal
3 Tbsp. Flour
2 Cups Buttermilk
1 Large Egg, beaten

Preheat oven to 350 degrees. Add fat to 10-inch cast iron skillet and place in oven to heat fat. Pour fat from skillet into cornmeal and mix. Stir in 1/2 of the buttermilk and egg. Add more buttermilk as needed. Pour the cornmeal mixture into hot skillet. Bake at 450 degrees for 20-25 minutes. Remove from oven and let rest. Turn onto plate.

Black Skillet Mammy's (Granny's) Little Baby Loves Short 'N Bread

1 1/2 Cups Sugar
3/4 Cup Butter, melted
2 Large Eggs
1 1/2 Cups All-Purpose Flour
1/2 tsp. Salt
1 tsp. Vanilla Extract

Preheat oven to 350 degrees. Line a 10-inch black skillet with foil and grease foil. In a large bowl mix sugar into melted butter. Beat the eggs in one at a time. Stir flour and salt into the batter. Add vanilla and stir well. Pour into skillet. Cook about 35 minutes. Cool shortbread in skillet before cutting.

Collection of Vignettes: Authored by each Aunt
Vignette is a French word that means "little vine."

Vignette #1   Aunt Linda King Ledford
Idylls of Pickens Hollow

Vignette #2   Aunt Linda King Ledford
Wheat Thrashing Day

Vignette #3   Aunt Linda King Ledford
Remembering Mooresville School

Vignette #4   Aunt Linda King Ledford
Recess and Dinner at Mooresville School

Vignette # 5   Aunt Carolyn Ledford Fortson
My Academic Prowess

Vignette #6   Aunt Betty Ledford Roberts
The Depths of the Great Depression

Vignette #7   Aunt Alice Ledford Foughner
Growing Tobacco in Middle Tennessee

Vignette #8   Aunt Alice Ledford Foughner
Fondest Memories

Vignette #1
Idylls of Pickens Hollow
Linda King Ledford

It started a long time ago for my parents, Ruth King and Bryan Ledford. They were married on January 28, 1921. Since my birthday is January 27, 1929, I was almost their eighth anniversary present. There were three births before mine, Gene, Tyson and Betty. We lived on the Marsh Place in the Wilson Hill Community in Marshall County, Tennessee.

I was four years old, and we were still living at the Marsh Place when Carolyn was born. I remember it very well. Children were born at home then. I was taken to Mrs. Knapton's when this blessed event took place. Later, William Knapton brought me home on his shoulders. When I spied this strange little car, a green and black top coupe, parked out front of our house, I knew something was up! After we had gone into the house, something had been added! There was a baby crib with a dark head peeping out from under the blanket. It was Carolyn Ruth! About a year later, we moved to Pickens Hollow in the Mooresville Community in Marshall County.

When we lived at the Marsh Place, there were no children around, so we amused ourselves playing in the barns, spring house and fields.

They told this on Tyson. One day, he chased a rabbit that had been shocked into a corn field. The rabbit ran under one stalk. Tyson set fire to it! Another tale, I remember this, it was supper time and about dark. Tyson was in trouble with our parents. He announces that he would leave home (he was about eight years old)! He stomped out the kitchen door and around the house. In the meantime, Daddy went through the dining room. As he went by, he grabbed the white tablecloth off the table, draped it over his head, went out the front door and around the house. Tyson met this white apparition head on! He turned and fled around the house and into the kitchen, falling in head first, yelling about a big, white thing in the yard! Leaving home didn't occur to him again.

One-time Betty and I, and I'm sure this was Betty's idea, decided we would ride Ole Maude, Pa's horse. Maybe we were about four and six years old. How we caught the horse and saddled her is not clear anymore. We were riding along and fell off! We had not fastened the saddle cinch. I looked at Betty, and there was blood on her face. I took my sun bonnet and wiped her face. We went to the house crying, leaving the poor horse standing there. What Mama did or said has escaped me now.

When we were still living at the Marsh Pace, I went to see my dear friends, the Knaptons, Belle, Mary Thomas and William, every day. They spoiled me rotten. This family was so dear to us, they were loved like family. We remained friends for over sixty years. Mr. Knapton and Daddy were the first tobacco farmers in the country. He taught Daddy how to raise tobacco.

Pickens Hollow, in the Mooresville Community, was home for me for more than twenty-five years. We had a lot of neighbors who had children for us to play with. The Ayers girls, Geneva, Frances and Helen were our dear friends. We played together almost every day. On summer days, we played in the creek or hiked into the woods. William Wilson, who lived nearby, and us children spent many hours exploring the cave on Mr. Ervin's place, the fields and the woods. William taught us how to ride a bicycle. Tyson and William were "big buddies." William, who lives in Lynnville, Tennessee with his wife Betty Jo, who was our neighbor in Pickens Hollow, are still dear friends, and we include them as part of our family.

At Christmas time, we would look for a cedar tree on the farm for our Christmas tree. We would walk and look until we found the perfect tree. When we got it home, hammered the boards on the trunk for a stand, took it into the house and it was bigger than we thought! We decorated it with whatever we had. Sometimes we hung sycamore tree balls sprayed with gold or silver paint on them. Mama decorated the mantle with cedar boughs and candles. We'd hang our stockings on Christmas Eve. Tyson and Gene would put out their caps. Santa usually left us "outing" pajamas, dolls, mittens, fruit, candy and raisins that were dried on the vine. We would get up early Christmas morning to see what Santa had left us. Mama cooked a traditional Christmas dinner - turkey, dressing, sweet potatoes, boiled custard, coconut cake and usually a jam cake. At Christmas time during the Depression, many families would cook four or five cakes. Not us! Mama didn't cook cakes too well. She did well to bake two! It was always fun to see her "kill the coconut." Coconuts with their big eyes always intrigued me! You saw coconuts only around Christmas time.

I don't remember too many white Christmases. When it did snow, usually at night, Mama and Daddy would be the first ones to discover it. Mama would be so excited. When we were young, we didn't have accurate weather forecasters. I remember one snow particularly. Tyson built a sled, hitched it to a horse, and we went sleigh riding in the neighborhood. What fun! Sometimes we would pull our homemade sled up on Pickens Hill for a ride downhill. Now, this was daring! We'd all pile on and someone would push, then jump on and down the hill we'd go! If it looked as if we were going to hit a tree or bush, the one in the front yelled "bail out!"

Our cousins from Nashville would come to visit during the summer. Aunt Tera Mann, Daddy's sister, and children, Melba, Doris and Thomas would come and visit for a week. With eight children in our household, there were many harrying moments. One event took place that stands out in my mind. Daddy had bee hives. These creatures flying in and out fascinated Thomas. Daddy told him not to touch the hives. Thomas, being Thomas, had to lift the top to see what was going on inside. Needless to say, what happened! He ran screaming to his mother.

While they were visiting, the boys would go blackberry picking. Thomas ate his berries, and when they got home, Tyson and Gene's bucket would be full. Thomas would tell his mother that Gene and Tyson took his berries! One time, Mary Ruth Ledford, Uncle Levoy and Aunt Yula, Mary's daughter, came to spend the night with us. The older ones, I wasn't included, went to the movies in Lewisburg. Mary Ruth convinced Gene she could drive. They ended up in the ditch! No harm done. In those days, cars didn't go too fast.

Gene and Tyson played football. Both were good players. One time, Gene and Tyson couldn't stay for after school practice. Coach Luna made them run the track. That was no problem to them. If anything, it was easier to them than practice. They were farm boys. They were tough. When he saw that it was easy for them, he put them back on the field. Daddy enjoyed going to see the boys play. One time after the game was over, Daddy, Judge Wallace, and Mr. Jones Rutledge were on the field discussing the game, and they were accidently locked in and couldn't get out. Daddy, being a big man, helped Mr. Rutledge over the fence to go for help. That was a big joke around town.

Our Grandfather, Anthony Smith "Pa" Ledford, lived with us all during his later years. He was a man loved and respected by all. He was a farmer and stockman, particularly mules. When Daddy was a young man, he'd take the mules to the fair in Nashville and stay all week. Some mules won prizes. Some images of Pa are still clear to me. He always kept candy, usually Milky Way bars, in his wardrobe. About ten o'clock in the morning, he'd get a bar, cut it into enough pieces for all us so each one would get a share. That little bite was "soooo" good.

He was always having an accident in the car. So, one day he drove the car through the "car shed" out into the garden. He had put the gear in forward instead of reverse. No damage was done to the car. The wall was pushed up and out, and the car went right under and out into the garden, and the wall flipped back into place. It upset him somewhat, and Mama drove the car out of the garden! We loved him.

The last two little girls were born at the Pickens Place. Amy and Alice were pretty, little blond-haired girls. We older ones loved them dearly. Gene was eighteen when Alice was born. Alice loved to ride the horse. Daddy would put her on the horse, and she was so small she could hardly hold on to the saddle. Daddy would lead the horse, with Alice hanging on, around and around in the front yard. She would cry when we'd take her off. Now, Amy loved the outdoors and everything on the farm. She followed Daddy around and knew everything that was going on at the farm. She kept up with it all. They were a lot of joy to us.

My thing was basketball. I started playing basketball at Mooresville School when I was in the fifth grade. One exciting time for me, I guess I was in the fifth or sixth grade, Mr. Mullins, our principal and coach, asked me to go and play with the team. Later, my freshman year at Marshall County High, I won the trophy for the most outstanding player that year, 1943. I played four years in high school. It wasn't easy to stay after school for practice and then get home about ten miles from school. I rode home with Gene after he got off from work. Many times, it was after dark when we'd get home. Tyson would meet me in Lewisburg after a road trip. I couldn't have done this without their help and my high school friends. I was a very good player and made honors in the sport!

I guess we kept the neighbors entertained. There were so many of us coming and going. We had parents who were always there for us and a good home to come home to. Our friends were always welcomed. Daddy was proud of us. Mama never let on, but she was proud, too. She'd say, "Do as well as you look."

One thing that was pointed out to me by William Wilson was Daddy let us take a checkbook to college. This wasn't a problem to us because we always knew how much we could spend.

We had a good life on that farm in Pickens Hollow, tucked away in the hills of Tennessee.

Vignette #2
Wheat Thrashing Day
Winter Wheat
Linda King Ledford

One of the most interesting days on the farm was wheat thrashing day. It takes a year's work by the farmers to reach this day. It all starts in the fall of the year. My father, Bryan, would prepare the field to be planted with winter wheat seeds. It would grow during the winter months. Now, this sounds odd for a crop to grow during the winter. Well, that's why it's called winter wheat. Daddy would welcome the snowfalls during the winter. He said the snow protected the young plants from the cold winter winds. It acts as a blanket.

When spring comes, the rain and warm sunshine make the plants grow until they mature in June. The plants are on a head, which contains grain. Now, when the plant turns a beautiful golden tan, it is time to cut the wheat. A very beautiful sight to see is a field of golden tan swaying in the wind over a lovely June day. In the days of yore, the garden was cut by hand with a sickle or a cradle scythe. During our time, it was cut by a machine called a binder.

Wheat cutting was a fun time, too. The machine would cut the stalks with heads on it. When the wheat went through the machines, it would make bundles of the stalks with the heads(grain) still intact. The bundles would be tied around the middle with turn strings. Men would come behind the binder and stack the bundles(sheaves) into shocks. A shock would have about five or so bundles stacked to make a mound, like a little hill. The shocks stayed in the field for several weeks until it dried. Then, it was ready to be thrashed.

The men who grew wheat helped each neighbor the day the thrasher came to their house. There would be as many as ten to twelve men who came to help out. They would come in their wagon train pulled by a pair of mules. The farmers stood tall and proud, wearing their overalls and straw hats and would drive into the fields to gather the shocks of wheat. The thrasher, a big machine, would already be there stationed in a spot where the wheat would be separated from the stalks. The thrasher was made of metal with a big chute that would blow the straw into a pile as big as a good size "hill." The wagons would pull up by the machine, and the men would throw the bundles or sheaves into the machine. The machine separated the grain from the stalk. The grain would go down a chute that emptied into a tow sack. A man stood there holding the sack until it was filled with the wheat grains. The stalks came out the other end through a big silver chute or pipe like structure. When the stacks were expelled through this pipe, it was then called straw. When the day or days were over there was a pile of straw as big as a good size hill or mound. The bags of wheat were stored in a building or wheat house for safe keeping until it was taken to market or a mill. Meanwhile, the ladies of the house would cook dinner for all the hands. As I said, it was an exciting day because everyone had a job to do. Mama and the women who lived on the place cooked dinner. We were too small to help out, but we still had our little jobs to do, too. Mama fried chicken and cooked vegetables out of the garden. There would be green beans, potatoes, green onions, etc. By that time, usually around the Fourth of July, blackberries would be ripe. We children picked the berries so Mama could make a blackberry cobbler. There would be iced tea to drink.

The men would come to dinner after they washed up at the spring. They would come into the kitchen, fill their plates and eat at the kitchen or dining room table. Some would go to the spring to eat. After mealtime, the men would go back to the fields, and the ladies would clean up the kitchen. That's when we girls helped.

We were not allowed to play on the straw stacks, until after it had rained several times. Daddy said the straw was not safe until it had packed down. Then we were allowed to roll and tumble on the straw stack. It was so much fun! We were not allowed to dig tunnels because it could collapse and suffocate us.

In the winter, cows would eat the straw like hay. People would use straw like it was feather. They would make straw beds, which were used on top of a mattress, or make straw pillows. We always had geese, so we always had feathers. The day Mama picked the geese was another fun day.

Daddy sold his wheat to a feed mill in town. Sometimes, he had the wheat ground into flour. Mama used it like any other flour. Of course, it wasn't as good as flour we have today. All the additives weren't in it.

Daddy had a load of wheat he had taken to Nora Miller. Some was to be made into flour. Daddy usually stood by watching all the action. He would make sure his wheat was used to make his flour. On this particular day, he had jury duty at the Court House, so he took Baxter Reed, who was hired to help Daddy on the farm, to watch the proceedings. He was told, "if you see anything going on that isn't right, go get the sheriff, John Evans." Sure enough, he saw that our good wheat wasn't used to make our flour! Baxter went to get Johnny! I'm sure Daddy didn't press charges because we had to deal with those people for many things relating to the farm. We all had a good laugh at Baxter.

Sometime, during the 40's maybe, a new machine replaced the binder. It was called a combine, a machine pulled by a tractor. This machine came into a field of grain, cut, thrashed and sacked the grain at the same time. When the machine had cut the grain, the work was complete in that field. The grain in sacks was picked up by truck and stored.

There was a local man in our community, Mooresville, who had a combine and tractor. His name was Howard Brandon. Howard did everybody's wheat. He worked day and night. He was honest and good at what he did. There are some people you never forget.

Daddy raised wheat for many years until something else took its place. Wheat required a lot of work to raise, but a certain amount of joy resulted in your efforts.

Vignette #3
Remembering Mooresville School
Linda King Ledford

As early as I can remember, someone I know was going to Mooresville School. In those days, the students rode their ponies to school, including my older brothers and sister. We were living on the Marsh Place in the Wilson Hill Community. Old Maude was saddled up for the daily trek to Mooresville School.

When I started school, we rode the school bus. I believe the first one I rode was a "blue" bus. The yellow one came soon after driven by hard-driver, Casey Jones. He was notorious to all who rode his bus. I think he drove for 50 years! He was tough on you if you moved. Later came Jim Beckman. There's a lot to remember about riding a bus to school for twelve years.

My first-grade teacher was Miss Maple McConnell. There were two grades in each room. She was the best. I remember she used flash cards, spelling bees, show and tell, a sand table and other means to teach us. The sand table usually had scenes depicting the seasons such as winter, Christmas and Easter.

There were about twenty to twenty-five students in a room. Recess time and lunch hours were filled with all sorts of things to do, play upon the hill, ball on the courts or across the road. Teachers were not out on the playground all the time. We played and made up our own games.

Mr. Mullins, a handsome young man, was one principal I remember the best. He taught me to play basketball. I started when I was in the fifth grade. I was always taller than the other girls. I was so excited when he asked if I could go on a basketball trip to play with the team. Mama and Daddy always let us do things like that. Some parents wouldn't let their girls go on trips, wear shorts, etc. From then on, I played basketball until I graduated from high school.

Mr. Mullins stayed at Mooresville School until World War II broke out. He left us to join the Marines. He wrote to us after he left. Can you imagine that? He did so many things with us. He'd take us over the hill to skate on a pond, and let us play basketball in the auditorium on cold winter days. I read in a publication from M. T. S. W. that he died in the summer of 1997.

Ms. Mary Woods Barnett was my third and fourth grade teacher. She was a beautiful person, pretty, peachy complexion and light brown hair. My favorite recall about her is her reading stories to us after lunch. Some of my favorites are Heidi, Aunt Minerva and William Green Hill and Uncle Wiggly. These stories were entertaining, and we all enjoyed listening to her read. Miss Barnett had a weight problem, but I didn't notice. That explains why she ate only an apple every day for lunch - a big, red, delicious apple. We all loved her.

Now, Miss Lowe was another story. She taught the sixth and seventh grade. I think some fifth graders failed so they wouldn't have to go into her room! I didn't go near her room, which was in the basement. I'd go the other way around the building. She was about six feet tall with red hair and a temper like we'd never seen. You learned because you were afraid not to. Some claimed she hit them with pokers! She was Ivan the Terrible of Mooresville School! Thank goodness she left when I was in the fifth grade. I'm afraid I'd have had a hard time with her.

Let me tell you about the heating system at Mooresville School. When I started school, about 1935, the building was heated with the big potbellied stove. Each room had one. If you were close to it, you were very warm, the others who were near the door were barely affected by it. They were always cold. The boys would keep the fire roaring all day. Usually two boys would go get the coal. Sometimes they would forget to come back. The teacher would send someone after them. Water was heated on the stove to wash our hands for lunch. In the fall and spring, the windows were raised, and a cool breeze passed through and kept everybody comfortable. Sometimes, in September, the rooms were quite warm, and we'd make a fan out of tablet paper. We'd fan away! When I came to teach at Mooresville School in the fall of 1949, it had the same heating and cooling system! We had a good time sitting around those old stoves, talking, playing games, reading and drying gloves and stockings after playing in the snow.

The water system was worse. There wasn't one. There was cistern. If it rained in the fall, we had water. Dry falls were bad news. We'd have to go down the road to a spring to get a bucket of water. We'd make paper cups out of notebook paper. The water didn't taste good, but it was wet!

When I started at Mooresville School, there were grades one through ten, I believe. I thought those high school students were so grown up. I don't remember the older students bothering or hurting us in any way.

There were plays put on by students during the year. That was a lot of fun! At Christmas time, we had trees in the room and exchanged gifts. Sometimes, we'd have one big tree in the auditorium for all.

My first two years of teaching were at Mooresville School. As I look back after teaching four decades, those two years were perhaps the best. I had third grade in one room, not bad. I still had about thirty students. They were special. Some were Alice, Nancy and Peggy Ledford and one boy I remember very well was Hugh Stacey, Jr.! They were all sweet children. We had a good time.

I was going to read them a story, so I started Lassie Come Home. I noticed right off that it was too sad a story to read to farm children.

Mooresville School was closed, like all country schools, not for better but for worse in a way.

Vignette #4
Recess and Dinner at Mooresville School
Linda King Ledford

Oh, boy! It's ten o'clock! Recess time! Time to take a break from lessons, reading, math, geography, etc. Time to be excused and time to run and play in the school yard. All grades one through eight had recess at the same time. The girls would all go up the hill behind the brick school house to the outdoor toilet, a six-holes one. The holes were graduated from small to large ascending to your size and grade. No individual stalls, all open. This was when little girls stood and stared at the older girls to see if they had anything the younger ones didn't have. The only game we played there was seeing who could hang the deepest and longest in the hole without sailing our feet!

After we attended to that business, we would run and play. One game was to choose sides and play "Andy-Over" the school building. Remember grades one through eight were playing together. The big boys would throw the ball over the school building, then we would all run. If you had a crush on an older boy or thought one was cute, you would try to get on his side. Since recess was a short break, it was soon time to return to our rooms for more lessons and wait for dinner time.

Dinner time was one hour long. We would eat our lunch quickly from our lunch boxes or wrapped in a bread wrapper and then rolled in a newspaper. The Ledfords did have newspapers because the "Nashville Tessessean" came every day, Depression or no Depression. We made "play houses" under the trees on the top of the hill behind the school building. We would bring broken glass from home for dishes and pick up rocks for furniture and dividing the house into rooms. You tried to outdo the group who was building one next to you. The boys would take the metal sides of a broken desk, put the sharp side down, and grade paths up and down the hill to the "play houses."

One of the most exciting days was when the big grades came to the campus and leveled us off a basketball court. A double one, one for boys and one for girls. Poles were cut, measured and erected for the four goals. We were coached, we became teams, we got blue and white suits, and we competed with other country teams - Chapel Hill, Belfast, Ostella, Culleoka and others. We thought we were worth a million when we were handed the suits. We had a good coach, hence, we won. As we moved onto high school, our coach followed us, and we were hard to handle.

We had a big, rather new brick school to attend. When the new school was built, which I don't remember, the county asked for volunteer labor and tools. Pa King, Mama's father, came to work and helped build the new school.

Vignette #5
My Academic Prowess
Carolyn Ledford Fortson

My memories of Mooresville School were when I was five years old. Mama had tried to start me in the first grade. I don't know if she thought I was big for my age or she could get me out of the house. The principal stood firm, and he announced that I to be six years old.

The school had no indoor plumbing or water. We would line up and drink out of spigots. The spigots were fed by a cistern. A student would crank the handle.

The school had four classrooms. There was first-grade in one, second grade in one and third, fourth and fifth in another. The older students through the eighth grade were in the last one. There was a small library with globes, maps and books.

We later had a cafeteria. There was an auditorium with a stage and curtain. This is where we had our plays, fund raisers and other school events.

Our mother rose in the morning, made a fire in the wood stove for breakfast and warmth. She made a half dozen lunches and packed them in time for us to catch the ole yellow school bus.

My daddy rose, went to the barn and fed the cattle. Then, he milked thirty or more cows.

Mr. Thomas was our bus driver, and he was mean and grouchy. He would certainly leave us if we were late. We would ride for miles before we got to school.

I remember Catherine Orr as my first-grade teacher. She looked like Barbie, and she wasn't much bigger than her first and second graders. She would bring her heels and let us play in them. She wore a 4 1/2 or 5 shoe, so they just fit our feet. My cousin, Ellen, and I had a good time wearing those shoes!

Catherine later married my cousin and Ellen's brother, Selwin Ledford. Our teachers all read to us because we had no videos to watch. They all loved us, but there was one teacher, Miss Lowe. Everyone was scared to death to go to the fifth grade. She left before I had the pleasure of being in her room!

The fall was an exciting time because we started back to school. The weeds would be over our heads. Today, parents would think this would be a health hazard or a safety issue. We played hide and seek in those weeds, and we rolled and played in those weeds until they were flattened.

We children played many games because we didn't have indoor courts, play equipment, etc. We had issued to us a basketball, softball and bats when school started.

The teachers let us go across the road to a field on private property. We chose sides and played together and settled our problems without a teacher. The boys brought their own pocket knives to play Mumble Peg. Those knives were wicked. The knives stayed in their pockets. The boys played marbles, and the girls played chase. We were just as silly as girls are today.

We didn't have computers, videos or television, but we were responsible, reliable and innovative. Our parents were home when the ole yellow school bus dropped us off from school. In the winter, it was dark when we got home, and it was dark when we left for school. These were good and simple times.

Our father had a stock farm, and he rose at dawn to start his day's work. Daddy had a modern dairy farm for the day. The floors and feeding bins were concrete. They had to be cleaned each day. He then took the cow manure and spread it on his fields. He would plant cover crops to put nitrogen in the soil, and he plowed this into the soil in the spring. My father was an organic farmer before it was politically correct.

We, as young children, had horses to ride. We all learned to ride at an early age. My sister, Betty, was crushed when one of the boys that lived and worked on our farm carved a face in her saddle. Saddles were expensive back then.

Summer vacation found us reading or making playhouses with the Ayers' children. We played in the creeks and I would slide down on the rocks. I would sit in the sun until my dress dried. Yes, I said dress. We did not wear shorts. Our mother made all of our dresses, bloomers, shirts and blouses on the ole Freddie sewing machine.

My mother put brown dresses on me, and I hate brown to this day. She would make our flannel gowns and pajamas for winter. We would get these for Christmas gifts.

I will focus on my early Christmas memories. The Ledford family which consisted of five sisters, Betty, Linda, Carolyn, Amy and Alice, and two brothers, Gene and Tyson. We lived in an old, large Greek Revival house called Pickens Place. The community was called Pickens Hollow for this old family. The old Dave Pickens' home was bought by my parents, Bryan and Ruth Ledford, to raise this large family. The house had two big double rooms that opened into a large hall with a big stairway going to the second floor. We had a huge kitchen which had been the dining room, with built in cabinets. The floors were poplar and had to be scrubbed and waxed. The house had no central heat or bathrooms. It was cold in the winter but cool in the summer.

My mother always decorated the big, beautiful mantles with red candles and greenery. She always put greenery beside our big, double front doors. She would use red tissue paper to fashion bows. You must remember this was before Wal-Mart and the big, red house bows we can buy today.

My job at Christmas was to go to our neighbors, the Pickens sisters, two little old maids that lived in one of the big Pickens' houses. They had pine trees in their yard. I would gather the cones and get pine greenery.

Lord knows what these little women lived on. This was before Social Security and Welfare.

The Jones' lived across the field from us and in later years had outside lights.

Going for the Christmas tree was a great adventure. We lived on a Christmas farm and didn't know that we were blessed. Moot, our hired hand, cut brush in the off season, but he left plenty of cedar trees. We girls often re-marked, "What Moot could have cleared if he had a chain saw." My sisters and I, armed with an ax, would set off for the tree. It would take hours to find one because one tree was as pretty as the next. They grew in the open and got plenty of sun, very full and fragrant. We would cut a tree much too big. We would drag it to the house and our father would cut the length and put it in a stand in the living room. It was so cold in the living room that it would stay fresh all year, but mother would not tolerate that idea.

We had plain decorations. This was during the war and there was not much in the stores. Sugar, butter, gas and shoes were rationed. There were so many children, and we all had our ration cards. We didn't suffer too much. Mama and Daddy did all their shopping on Christmas Eve. Christmas wasn't so commercialized back then. With a war on, even cloth was scarce. We always had hard candy, dried fruit and fresh fruit. We didn't have bananas be-cause they were shipped from the tropics!

We hung our stockings on the end of the bed. We had beautiful mantles, and we were not allowed to nail nails into the wooden mantles. I have since read that was an old English or Scottish custom.

There were so many of us that we would get two gifts and our stockings stuffed. I would get a doll dressed in pink while Linda's was dressed in blue. I remember leaving my doll in the rain, and she lost her head and arms. We would have jam cake, coconut cake and boiled custard with bourbon. We would have all the Christmas parties at our house because Ruth had the big house. We would make wood fires in all the fireplaces, and the cedar would smell so good. Our brothers would bring the wild holly and mistletoe.

This is the winter season so I must tell you about hog killins. My father, with the men that lived on our farm, would kill their hogs around Christmas. This time of year would bring our first cold weather. There had to be cold weather because the meat would spoil. This was before freezer lockers. There was a big smoke house on our farm which had a fire pit on the first floor. There would be a fire in this pit, and the smoke would go between the slotted boards that made the second floor. They would smoke the meat for days. My father did not use this method. He used a sugar cure, and he would rub his meat for days with this mixture.

The hogs were killed and hung to get all the blood removed. They were put in hot, scalding water to remove hair. The meat was cut and salted. Mama would cut the fat from the meat. This was put in a big, black pot over a hot fire, and it was cooked down for the lard. The lard was stored in large containers. Lard was used for cooking purposes.

My father cut up meat and ground the sausage. He had a special blend of herbs and spices for seasoning. Everyone would be very tired after hog killing because butchering was a big job. This was just one of the many jobs on a big farm.

Vignette #6
The Depths of the Depression
Betty Ledford Roberts

In August 1932, the depth of the Great Depression, people were desperate, losing their homes and farms, being uprooted, no jobs, no food! But life had to go on, so it was on the Marsh Place in Globe Hollow Community, Marshall County, Tennessee.

A third sibling of Bryan and Ruth Ledford, I was about to embark upon a tenure of "going to school" which would last for forty-nine years. Back to the most pressing problem of the moment, how was Betty going to get to and from school at Mooresville, a distance of about five miles, every day. No school buses in the dark ages! You see, our pretty pony had died from an accident. Running from the larger horses, she had stuck a stub into her chest which went to her heart. The vet came, medication was applied by Daddy and Pa Ledford but to no avail. It was a sad morning when Mama came to the Chapman folding bed where Linda and I were sleeping and told us the horse had died during the night.

Fortunately, the first-grade teacher, Miss Mary Wilson, lived up the road from us and would pass our house every day. She agreed to let me ride with her for a small fee. However, as the year progressed, and she had to stay for teacher's meeting, go to town and other after-school involvements, it became evident that this situation was not satisfactory. There was no other alternative except for little sister to ride on the saddle mare, Maude, with the older brothers. Gene, the older, in the saddle, Tyson on the behind. I was put in the middle behind Gene in the saddle and Tyson on the back, far back! So here we go every morning - hot, cold, rain, sleet, snow! Daddy, Pa, some of Aunt Ollie's or Uncle Zet's family would saddle-up our horse each morning, and bring her to the house.

When we reached the main road, which ran by the school, Mary Ruth Ledford, our cousin, Clyde Jr., Gene's seatmate at school, joined us for our daily trek. Ole Maude with Gene in front, Betty in the middle, Tyson on the back, Clyde Jr. on his fishy pony and Mary Ruth walking. Mama said, "Levoy should be a shamed making Mary Ruth walk to school."

There were stables at school joined all in a row for the horses and ponies to stay in during the day while the students were in their classrooms. Hay was carried by each family and put in the stables for the animals to eat during the day. But no water!

I had a new tin dinner box to carry my dinner in every day. Usually a biscuit and ham, piece of fried chicken or steak, cucumber pickle or a tomato in the fall. I was so proud of my dinner box with circus themed pictures all around it.

One afternoon when I got home, I realized that I had forgotten my little dinner box. I was so worried, but the next morning when we got to our stable, Bruce Pigg, who had the stable next to us, had seen my dinner box and had set it in our stable. Was I relieved? Yes!

Snow began falling one cold winter day. By the time school was out and we were on our way home, the ground and road was covered with wet slippery snow. As we were going down a small rise below the house where Mary and Al lived, Ole Maude's back feet slipped under her. Tyson slid off her back and pulled me off. We were not injured. Gene got off and helped us back upon our horse, and we were soon home warming by the fire in an open fireplace.

During my year in second grade, the Ledford family moved from the Marsh Place at Globe to the Pickens Place in Pickens Hollow. Marshall County was making progress, money was available for school buses. Of course, the Democrats had been victorious, and FDR had been elected President of the U.S. This ended my horse-riding days to school.

Vignette #7
Growing Tobacco in Middle Tennessee
Alice Ledford Foughner

My father was one of the first farmers to grow tobacco in Marshall County, TN. He was taught by a man who came from Kentucky and brought his family during the Great Depression. The family was walking down the road by our home and asked if we had a place where they could live. My father agreed and told them to remove the grain from the grain house to make a home. The Knapton's lived on our place for a long time. Their family did very well and are still living in the Murray County area of Tennessee near Columbia.

Tobacco is grown in the early spring from seed. Farmers would find a good plot of land 40 feet long by 10 feet wide and burn wood on it to kill weeds and insects and create fertilizer. Afterwards, they would plow up the ground and plant seeds. The tobacco bed would have logs around it and a canvas top to protect the seeds.

When the soil is ready, the workers drop the plants about 2 1/2 feet apart and someone comes along and uses a stick to punch a hole in the soil with water. The amount of tobacco you could grow was given to you by the government. Tobacco growth was monitored, and one could not grow as much as they wanted. Later, they had machines to set the tobacco out. The setter had a place for two people. They sat side by side and put plants into the machine, and it also provided the water.

You have to plow to keep the weeds from growing. As the tobacco plants grow, you have to pull suckers, or extra growth, off the main stalks of the plant. You cut tobacco in the late summer. It is placed on a tobacco stick which is about 1 yard long. Then you hang it in the tobacco barns. These are the same as stock or milk barns.

The barn we used on Tyson's farm was built by the German POW's. As a little girl, I remember looking out the window and seeing the POW's go by in a truck. They would stop by the store in Mooresville, and the neighbors would buy them drinks.

Our family had a little shed which included a wooden stove for warmth and to strip the tobacco because it came "into case" to be stripped in January or February. The shed had a lot of windows to let the natural light in. This is needed to divide the tobacco into different grades. My father would sell the tobacco, and that would provide us money for late winter and spring.

Vignette #8
Fondest Memories
Alice Ledford Foughner

I am the seventh child and fifth daughter of Ruth King Ledford and Bryan Herman Ledford. I was born November 9, 1940. Some of my fondest memories are being at home with my mother and father when the rest of the children were in school. My father would put me on "Old Dolly" and lead her to the mailbox and back for me to get to ride. I would play upstairs in our house in my older sister's dresses.

My very early fears were during the second World War. I remember my older brother, Gene, taking me out for a walk in the field to the cow barn and explaining that he was going to have to go to a faraway place for a long time. He was in the Pacific during the war. I remember when he came home and how excited we all were. Mother cooked everything for him - country ham, fried chicken and fried apples. He was sick and malnourished.

My father had a large working farm - milk cows, hogs, horses and sheep. He grew crops, corn, wheat, oats and tobacco. Tobacco was a crop that provided money during the winter months. He usually sold tobacco in January or February. During this time, the cows did not produce much milk and money was tight. But Mother would have canned enough food for us to have during the winter. We had killed our beef and put it in a freezer locker. This was before freezers. We had a smoke house with plenty of pork, ham, shoulder and sausage.

My family has asked me to write about a time on the farm that was one of the most exciting times. This was when we used to get the sheep sheared. It was usually during May because you wanted to do the shearing before it became too hot in the summer. My father usually raised anywhere from 65-75 head of sheep. A lot of times, it was my job to go on the hill behind our house and bring the sheep up every night to keep the wild dogs from killing them. I guess you could call me a shepherd. My father would call the Miser brothers to come and shear the sheep. They would tell him they would be there on a certain date and time. The night before we would put the sheep in the lower barn to contain them until the brothers came. My father would be up early to milk the cows, and he would want everyone else up because the sheep shearers were coming, but of course they never got there early. It would be 10:30 or 11:00, and my father would have walked and looked down the road a million times. They would be getting hot in the barn. What to do? Finally, they would appear in a little black, flat-bed truck that looked like a model A with the shearing equipment on the back.

The brothers looked like a traveling comedy show. They would get out their clothes that they wore when they sheared the sheep. They had large, brown cloth sacks that the wool was packed into to take to market and sell. Tyson's job was to pack the long sacks. At the end of the day, he would be so oily from the lanolin off of the wool, that we said he could run and slide for a mile on his stomach.

45

The shearers would take each sheep, and begin at their stomach, making long strides up and down and then on their back. They would do their legs and shear the head last. When they finished, if they had nicked the sheep while shearing, they would put pine tar on the wound to keep it clean from bacteria and flies. The poor old sheep would feel so naked after losing her wool. They looked as if they wanted to run and hide because they were embarrassed without their wool coat. We usually got about three or four big wool bags full from our sheep. It would take all day and Mother had dinner for everyone at noon time - beef roast or fried chicken and maybe the first peach cobbler from our peach orchard. Mother would have a peach or blackberry cobbler every day. What great memories there are for our family!

Animals Raised on Ledford Land

1. Horses
2. Mules
3. Ponies
4. Jacks
5. Colts
6. Milk Cows
7. Beef Cattle
8. Calves
9. Heifers
10. Hogs
11. Pigs
12. Boar
13. Sheep
14. Lambs
15. Dogs
16. Cats
17. Chickens
18. Turkeys
19. Guineas
20. Ducks
21. Geese
22. Mice
23. Fish
24. Turtles
25. Snakes
26. Pigeons
27. Bees
28. Quail
29. Rabbits
30. Squirrels
31. Mink
32. Racoon
33. Skunks
34. Fox
35. Opossum
36. Song Birds

Plants and Crops Raised on Ledford Land

1. Wheat
2. Corn
3. Rye
4. Barley
5. Soy Beans
6. Tobacco
7. Lespedeza
8. Pumpkins
9. Milo
10. Cotton
11. Peanuts
12. Peaches
13. Carrots
14. Marigolds
15. Petunias
16. Timber – Cedar
17. Beets
18. Spirea
19. Walnut
20. Mint
21. Apples
22. Pears
23. Plums
24. Grapes
25. Persimmons
26. Raspberries
27. Strawberries
28. Blackberries
29. Cabbage
30. Lettuce
31. Onions
32. Radishes
33. Tomatoes
34. Zinnias
35. Timothy Grass
36. Timber-Hardwood
37. Coleus
38. Lilac
39. Cucumber
40. Watercress
41. English Peas
42. Sweet Potatoes
43. Irish Potatoes
44. Turnip Greens
45. Turnips
46. Mustard
47. Field Peas
48. Squash
49. Gourds
50. Watermelon
51. Iris
52. Sweet Peas
53. Oats
54. Alfalfa
55. Roses
56. Hawthorne
57. Bermuda Grass
58. Poke Salad
59. Blue Grass

People Who Lived on the Farm

1. Uncle Bob Fitzpatrick
2. Aunt Elda
3. Frog
4. Ivey
5. Phyllis
6. Uncle Zeterick Hill
7. Aunt Ollie
8. Grace
9. Dave
10. Pauline
11. Eudora
12. Pete
13. Odie Brown
14. Mr. Knapton
15. Mrs. Knapton
16. Amry Thomas
17. Belle
18. William
19. Duke Edwards
20. Russie Edwards
21. Henry Edwards
22. Mary Lee Edwards

23. Mr. Higdon
24. Mrs. Higdon
25. John Higdon
26. Lois Higdon
27. Baby Higdon
28. Mr. Cook
29. Mrs. Cook
30. Willard Cook
31. Jack Cook
32. Caliborne Higdon
33. Mrs. Parks
34. Robert Parks
35. Sidney Parks
36. Jay Dee Parks
37. Jennifer Mae Parks
38. Baxter Parks
39. Mary Nola Parks
40. Lucile Parks
41. Bird Parks
42. Bud Parks
43. Will Ed Parks
44. Louise Parks

45. William Lee Collier
46. Edna Collier
47. Wanda Collier
48. Wilson Hooten
49. Anna Hooten
50. Andrew Hooten
51. James Hooten
52. Eugene Hooten
53. Bobby Hooten
54. Mr. Wilson
55. Mrs. Wilson
56. James Whitfield
57. Ernie
58. Bobby
59. Barbara Wilson
60. Mr. Connie Gilliam
61. Mrs. Gilliam
62. Barbara Gilliam
63. Son Gilliam
64. Mr. Beck
65. Sister Ms. Beck
66. Mrs. Helmantalle

People Who Lived on the Farm

67. Homer
68. Peral
69. Shine
70. Mr. Shrader
71. Mrs. Shrader
72. Mildred
73. Berniece

74. Mr. Wintzel
75. Mrs. Wintzel
76. Vernell Wintzel
77. Margaret Wintzel
78. Marie Wintzel
79. Mr. Church

80. Ernest Church
81. Dee Ernest
82. Belle Church
83. Lloyd Church
84. Josephine Church
85. Catherine C. Powers

Mother of the Aunts
Mrs. Ruth Ledford

Ruth, or "Miss Ruth," as she was known to us, was an only child born to Sanford J. King and Carrie Duncan King of Marshall County on a farm in what is known today as the Rambo Hollow. This was on August 6, 1901.

She attended school at Duncanville, Mooresville and Haynes-McClean in Lewisburg, Tennessee. She rode her pony to school. One day the pony reared up with her, and a young boy came to her rescue. She was a tom-boy, enjoying riding horses and won a ribbon for the best show pony when she was sixteen. She also played basketball. She was tall, thin and pretty.

She married Bryan Herman Ledford in 1921. This was the man, who as a young boy, rescued her from her pony at school. At that time, they didn't know each other. She always said she wanted a big family when she married. So, to this union was born two sons and five daughters. They lived in the Wilson Hill community.

Thus, she embarked upon her career of being a wife, mother and homemaker. She always enjoyed good health and very seldom complained of feeling badly, not even a headache. This proved to be a great asset because her many daily tasks required much time and energy. She took time to sit with family at night after the evening meal.

Her children say she helped very little with their homework. When their first child entered school, his teacher was a very capable one and was our very own Mrs. Mary Tate Evans. Mrs. Evans advised them to let him become an independent student and so they took that advice with their other children. They were always supportive of their children's teachers and were taught they were always right and not to bring stories home about them. They were supportive of their children in school and urged them to attend college, especially the father. All the daughters except one have finished college and this one has three years completed. The sons were caught up in World War II. Gene went on to serve in the South Pacific Theater. As was the rule at the time, Tyson stayed to help run the farm. Ruth was the president of the first P.T.A. at Mooresville School.

Ruth was a member of the Lewisburg Baptist Church, but when they lived in Mooresville, she attended Mooresville Methodist Church. She was an active member of the Missionary Society and had them in her home for meetings.

Another important phase of her life was election day. Both she and her husband worked in the election polls, and the children went along and at times they worked too, like handing out flyers and voting cards for the candidates. They taught their children the importance of the day, and it was their duty to vote and be aware of the political climate of the day. They were staunch Democrats and were proud of it.

She probably was one of the charter members of the Mooresville Home Demonstration Club. She often quoted

Miss Mary Stanfil to her daughters. She remained a member of the club until her health kept her at home. She enjoyed the club and learned and practiced many new things in her home as a busy homemaker. The friendships she formed in the club remained with her through her life. The last time she attended was at Mrs. Evelyn Whitesell's for our Christmas party, and she said if was one the happiest days of her life. She was a member of the Marshall County Historical Society in her later years.

She sold the farm after the death of her husband and moved to Lewisburg, Tennessee on Scenic Drive where she lived the rest of her life.

As her children married, her daughters-in-law and sons-in-law were welcomed into the family and were loved as her own. Love and respect were reciprocated and mutual.

She enjoyed going but wanted to be home by dark. She loved her family and home and they were the center of her life. Visitors were always welcomed, and many shared her hospitality as the children's friends were often there at night and on weekends. Her children claim that she could always have a meal ready no matter what time they arrived or how far they had traveled. She possessed a warm personality. She was always cheerful, happy and fun-loving. She loved everyone. The primary things of her life were her children and concern for her family. Other things were trivial. She was a strong person who stood firm through the storms and turbulence of life. She was a mother, grandmother and great grandmother. Her children praise her. Her children loved her and cared for her. "Miss" Ruth was a good mother and a good wife. She was a good neighbor and friend. Our club has fond memories of her, and we cherish her friendship and memory.

The Mooresville Home Demonstration Club paid tribute and honor to her with a memorial rose given to the family of Ruth King Ledford on November 1, 1984.

Epilogue

Although the Aunts have now gone many miles and years from Pickens Hollow, we hope to preserve a slice of life to share with others. It is our hope that in reading about our recalled memories of a past time, that you might be heartened to lay down words of your own.

There was not always a complete victory as hoped for at each day's end on the farm, but victory was won in the end. After all, the Aunts were upon the land they loved so deeply. And how do I know this? My father was their brother.

About the Author
and
Artistic Contributor

Author

This book was a labor of love. A graduate from Georgia State University, Deborah Ledford Woodard, hails from Atlanta. The author now resides in beautiful Orange Beach, Alabama and loves living in an area where sunsets are coral and gold. She would like to wish her readers "Palm trees and sunshine to you."

Artistic Contributor

Dena McKee is an artist from Dauphin Island, Alabama who specializes in landmark paintings. Her paintings can be found in shops throughout the Gulf Coast and her work in collections around the country. Dena is a longtime family friend of the book's author and an admirer of her writing.